MW00711611

65 PRICELESS PROMISES

65 *Priceless* PROMISES

BISHOP T.D. JAKES

65 Priceless Promises Devotional

Copyright © 2022 T.D. Jakes Ministries

Printed in the United States of America.

ISBN: 978-1-951701-23-9

Assembled and Produced for T.D. Jakes Ministries by
Breakfast for Seven
2150 E. Continental Blvd., Southlake, TX 76092.
breakfastforseven.com

RESISTANCE IS LIFE

Fear is the number one enemy we face in this life. We must learn to push back against the seduction of fear if we are going to receive and walk in what God has for us. Think of your life as a blank canvas and faith and fear are what you choose to color your world.

Fear's objective is to paint your mind with negativity, so you see your life from a warped perspective. While fear causes us to connect to an undesirable outcome, faith will cause us to rise higher and higher like a skyscraper. When you tap into the voice of God, your faith is strengthened as you begin to see life from God's vantage point.

Don't allow externalities to determine your decisions. A storm arriving doesn't change what God promised you. His purpose for you is determined, and His Word is unchangeable. Don't stop believing. Remember, the race is not to the strong or the swift. The person who trusts in the Lord more than they believe the enemy's reports of fear will see God's glory manifest on their behalf!

I submit to the faith of God and resist the enemy's spirit of fear. God is leading me to a positive destination. I believe I receive the fulfillment of His promise in my life. I paint the canvas of my life with the Word of God. With the help of the Holy Spirit, my life becomes the masterpiece it was always intended to be. Amen.

. . . Thy daughter is dead; trouble not the Master. But when Jesus heard it, he answered him, saying, Fear not: believe only, and she shall be made whole.

LUKE 8:49–50, KJV

DYNAMIC FAITH

2

KEEP ON BELIEVING

The crisis of faith is a critical point when we must decide if we are going to keep believing Jesus or give in to fear. It's challenging when you are in a faith battle, and the pressure intensifies. At some point we'll all face a crossroads when it looks like the thing we prayed for and believed for has died.

What do we do when that happens? One secret this verse lets us in on is positioning. Jairus was with Jesus when he found out his daughter was dead. Even when the worst thing imaginable happens, it's always best to be in the presence of Jesus.

On the day when it looks like the sun has set on what you're believing for and fear is digging its claws into your soul, make sure you run to Jesus' presence. No matter how bad it looks, in His presence, He will give you the spiritual fortitude to keep standing for what He has already promised.

Lord, I thank You for Your finished work and for every promise You've given me by Your grace. Your blood purchased the right to come boldly before Your perfectly timed help. I need You, Lord. Help me to keep believing You in the face of fear. When it looks like my answer has died, I believe I will still see Your glory. Amen.

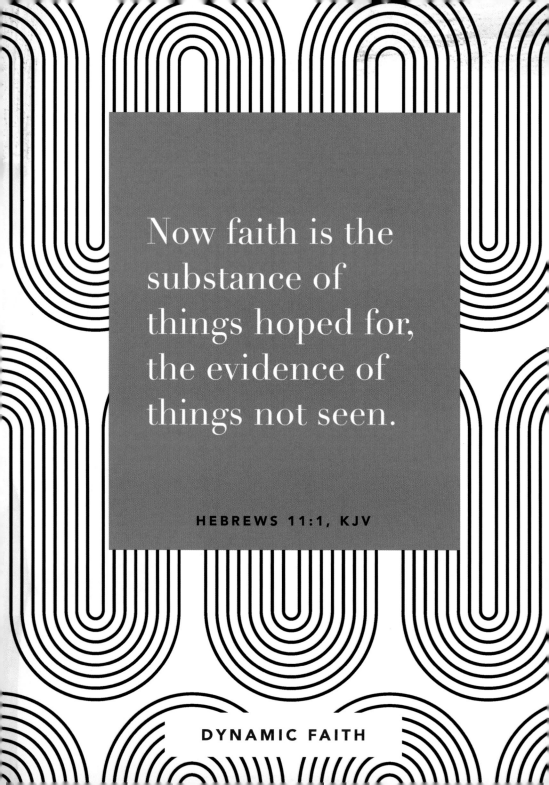

Now faith is the substance of things hoped for, the evidence of things not seen.

HEBREWS 11:1, KJV

DYNAMIC FAITH

SEEING THE UNSEEN

The simplicity of this verse should not be overlooked. There are so many misconceptions about what faith is and what it is not. Faith is not a cosmic force that can't be discerned. Faith is not invisible; it can be seen. Faith is substance. It is the building materials for the things we expect from God.

Faith is what God speaks. Your life may look contrary to what God has promised. Walking by faith means believing God's promises for you despite the lack of supporting evidence in your circumstances.

Even if you can't see any signs of what God has spoken to you, the promise is real. From a spiritual perspective, everything God said is already complete. He just needs someone to believe what He has spoken more than what their five physical senses tell them.

The thing you are hoping for is real. Your belief in what God said is your faith that gives substance and provides the building blocks of what can't be seen. Your breakthrough is coming. Take your eyes off the negative and look at your life through God's eyes to bring the unseen into reality.

What God has spoken in His Word and to me, specifically, is my faith. I believe the finished work of Jesus and my hope in the Lord will not be cut off. All the evidence I need is what God has promised. Lord, help me to keep believing even in times of uncertainty when it looks like my expectation in You is delayed. Just because I can't see it doesn't mean it's not real. Amen.

And Jesus said to them, "I am the bread of life. He who comes to Me shall never hunger, and he who believes in Me shall never thirst."

JOHN 6:35, NKJV

DYNAMIC FAITH

THE SATISFIED LIFE

We were created to live a fulfilling and satisfying life. Yet, we live in a world where many suffer from feelings of unfulfillment. With the spread of social media and the internet, we now have more reasons to be dissatisfied as we look at everyone else's highlight reel and compare their lives to our own.

Jesus knew He was the only One who could fill our void. The world beckons us to indulge ourselves in false substitutes to fill up the holes in our souls. It's never enough. There is no amount of money, entertainment, food, sex, drugs, or work we could engage in that could do what Jesus has promised.

He wants to fill you up. He won't force you to receive His filling. Instead, He has extended an eternal invitation to you. Go to Him and watch Him fill your hunger and quench your thirst. Spending time with Jesus on a regular basis will help you overcome feelings of lack and boredom.

Be proactive. Don't wait until you feel empty to go to God. Going to Him regularly will help you stay restful, at peace, and fulfilled in the joy of the Lord.

Lord, I believe You are the bread of life. I eat of Your Word and Your presence. I believe in You, and I draw near to you. I have no might in my own ability to satisfy myself. I need the real thing. I have Jesus, and He satisfies my hunger and quenches my soul's thirst.

Then Jesus told him, "Because you have seen me, you have believed; blessed are those who have not seen and yet have believed."

JOHN 20:29, NIV

DYNAMIC FAITH

BLESSED BELIEVING

Jesus spoke these words to the disciple Thomas after He rose from the dead and appeared to His disciples. When Thomas first found out Jesus was alive, He refused to believe it until he could see the wound marks on His body. When Jesus encouraged Him to touch Him and see for himself, Thomas was stunned. Jesus' loving rebuke is a healthy reminder for us today. In the world's system, seeing is believing. God's higher way dictates the exact opposite. In God's kingdom, believing is seeing.

Jesus was looking into the future and saw you believing in His Word without having His physical presence as the disciples did. There is a blessing He has reserved just for you. Something powerful happens when you take Jesus at His Word without the support of anything else. You come to know and trust Him as He proves His faithfulness to you.

Even after Jesus' resurrection, He met two of His disciples walking down the road to Emmaus. He restrained their eyes from recognizing Him (Luke 24:16). It wasn't until after He explained the prophets and Scriptures to them that their eyes were opened.

God wants you to know Him based on His Word, which is the starting point an intimate relationship. It would be thrilling if Jesus showed up at the foot of my bed with a word, but we don't need to see Him physically to know, believe, and manifest His glory.

My life is not ruled by my five physical senses. I discern and believe God based on His Word to me and our intimate relationship. Even though I can't see You, and many times I don't feel Your presence, I know You are with me. Thank You for the blessing of believing You beyond the sensory realm.

"Therefore I say to you, whatever things you ask when you pray, believe that you receive *them*, and you will have *them*."

MARK 11:24, NKJV

DYNAMIC FAITH

EFFECTIVE PRAYER

How do you approach God in prayer? As believers, we'd all like to say we approach God in faith when we pray, but many times we don't. Sometimes our religious tradition drives us, and we pray to earn from God rather than relating to Him. Other times, fear drives us, and we run to God as a last resort Hail Mary.

Our posture must change. God wants you to come near in prayer. He wants you to ask Him for the things you want with confidence. When you pray to the Father in the name of Jesus in accordance with God's will, believe you receive the answer the moment you pray. This is what it means to walk by faith.

When Jesus made these remarks about prayer, He knew we'd be challenged with doubt. A lot of times, we think we're believing God, but deep down, we're actually waiting to see evidence that our prayer "worked."

The key is to believe you have it when you pray. This confidence can only come from the intimacy of knowing your Father can't lie. You may not see your answer today, but from heaven's perspective, it's finished. Rest knowing it's only a matter of time before your answer manifests before your eyes!

I believe I receive the answer to my prayers when I pray according to Your will for my life. Help me to rest in confidence, knowing I have my answer even though I can't see it. I trust You, Lord.

If you have the FAITH to believe it, you have the POWER to conceive it!

BISHOP T.D. JAKES

DYNAMIC FAITH

BIRTHING YOUR DREAM

Religion tells us to focus on externalities while the Lord looks inward. He is more focused on your posture in faith. He wants you to give birth to the wonderful destiny He has for your life. The power to bring your dream to life comes from believing what God has revealed to you.

It doesn't take faith to believe something that is inside your comfort zone. God's vision will cause you to believe beyond your limitations. He wants you to believe Him to show you over-the-top goodness.

What has God been whispering in your ear that the enemy wants you to believe is too big to happen for you? I want you to know it's real. You serve a big God, and it's your time to see the end of your faith. Believe He wants to show you His goodness and bring the vision He's placed in your heart to life.

In the name of Jesus, I will give birth to the vision God gave me. I believe Jesus has empowered me to manifest His promises in my life. I believe in Jesus' finished work. I receive the end of my faith in Jesus' name.

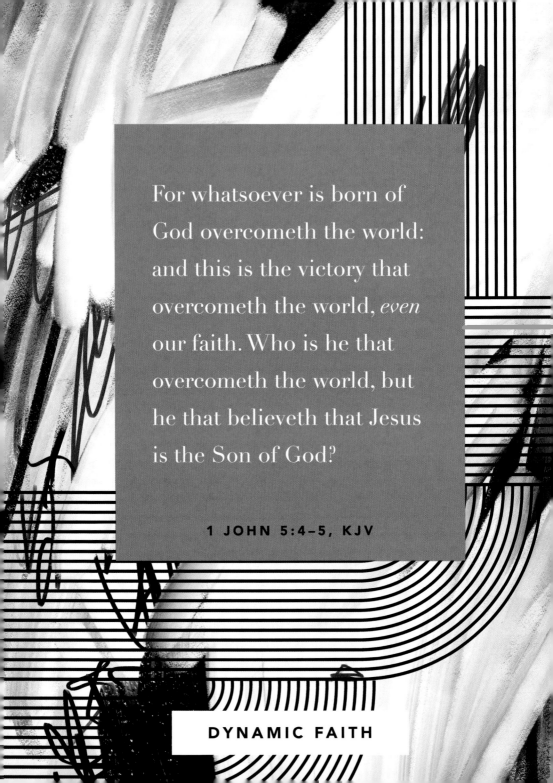

For whatsoever is born of God overcometh the world: and this is the victory that overcometh the world, *even* our faith. Who is he that overcometh the world, but he that believeth that Jesus is the Son of God?

1 JOHN 5:4–5, KJV

DYNAMIC FAITH

AN OVERCOMING LIFE

The world, the flesh, and the devil are our opposition. As believers, we've already been given the key to victory before the battle ever showed up. God declares you an overcomer in Him because you've been born again in Christ.

Being reborn in Jesus is what empowers you to overcome every test and trial that comes against you. Your faith in Jesus as your Savior is your victory. Knowing Jesus is the pinnacle of your life experience. To know Him is to know victory. So many in this world put their faith in everything else, but you chose to follow the man who came here to reveal the truth of the Father.

You are marked to live an overcoming life. You won't feel like it some days, but your outward condition doesn't diminish the spiritual truth that you have been made more than a conqueror because of the blood of Jesus. Amen.

I believe Jesus is the Son of God. I've received Him as my Savior, which means I overcome the world, the flesh, and the devil. Jesus is the conquering king, and I will walk in the victory He gave me through His death and resurrection. I triumph in all things in Jesus' name.

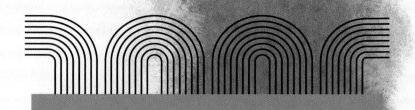

"He who believes in Him is not condemned; but he who does not believe is condemned already, because he has not believed in the name of the only begotten Son of God."

JOHN 3:18, NKJV

DYNAMIC FAITH

NO CONDEMNATION

Condemnation is the enemy of our souls. It's the weapon the enemy uses to keep us feeling unworthy of God's love. The only way to defeat condemnation is to believe in Jesus. He is the One who shed His blood for your sin. You've been washed of your sin, and now there is no blockage between you and God. Jesus tore the wall of sin and condemnation down that separated you from God's goodness.

The Holy Spirit in you will continue to reveal the truths about you being made righteous because of what Jesus has accomplished. Your belief in God's forgiveness will keep you safe from condemnation's onslaught. Meditate on God's Word regularly to fortify yourself before the test ever shows up.

The enemy wants to use your human weaknesses and areas you struggle in to make you feel you're no longer fit to be loved or used by God. Refuse to embrace his warped perspective. Take up the shield of faith and quench every fiery dart of condemnation that the enemy hurls at you.

I am not condemned. Jesus bore my sin on the cross and was condemned in my place. Now I stand justified before the Lord. Thank You, Lord, for making Jesus my righteousness and sanctification. I believe in the Son of God, and I am changed!

I pray that out of his glorious riches he may strengthen you with power through his Spirit in your inner being, so that Christ may dwell in your hearts through faith. And I pray that you, being rooted and established in love, may have power, together with all the Lord's holy people, to grasp how wide and long and high and deep is the love of Christ, and to know this love that surpasses knowledge—that you may be filled to the measure of all the fullness of God.

EPHESIANS 3:16–19, NIV

DYNAMIC FAITH

EMPOWERED BY LOVE

When the apostle Paul prayed for believers, He focused on God's abundant nature. Notice how he referenced God's glorious riches. This knowledge emboldened Paul when he prayed for the church. He was inspired by the Spirit of God to testify of the strength you were called to walk in centuries ago. His inspired words are still profitable for you today.

Paul's letter to the Ephesians reveals that it is the Holy Spirit who empowers you from within and is why Jesus is alive and dwelling in you right now. Think of that. You are one with the Almighty's indwelling presence. This kind of proximity births intimacy. And the closer you grow to the Lord, the more you will become rooted in His eternal love.

Allow this process to work in your life. Refuse the fleshy inclination to live life in a rush. Relating to God requires a crockpot, not a microwave. The more you fellowship with God, over time, your foundation of love gets stronger. The best part is that you don't have to rely on your own strength to accomplish this. The Spirit in you will help you to come to know the empowering love of God.

I receive a God-sized portion of strength from heaven's glorious riches. Father, thank You for the gift of the Holy Spirit living on the inside of me, who teaches me everything I need to know about Jesus. I am edified through relationships as I come to know the perfect love of God. Amen.

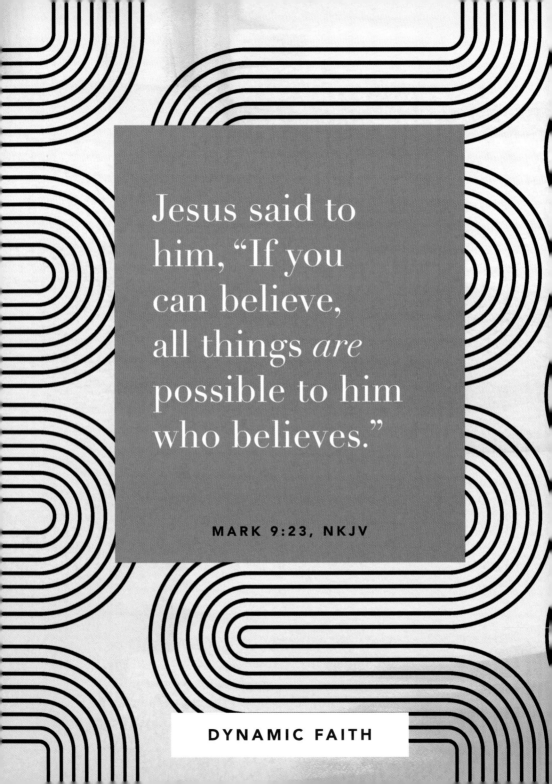

Jesus said to him, "If you can believe, all things *are* possible to him who believes."

MARK 9:23, NKJV

DYNAMIC FAITH

DOING THE IMPOSSIBLE

Jesus spoke this promise when comforting a distraught father whose child was having demonic epileptic seizures. His words are equal parts soothing and revolutionary at the same time. It reveals His relentless disposition when it comes to the work of the enemy.

As believers, we have to make one distinction with this promise. Jesus wasn't saying anything is possible. In context, He was referring to God's will. If we are going to be people who live and act in the name of the Lord, our first step is locating God's desire and purpose.

Jesus' belief is on display and has a twofold focus. First, Jesus knew and believed it wasn't His Father's will for a child to be tormented by a demon. Second, He believed He had the power to do something about it.

We are to do the same. When we are confronted with the work of the enemy, we must know and believe that God wants the work of the enemy destroyed and for people to be free. Knowing God's will gives us the boldness to operate in God's supernatural power, which will cause us to overcome limitations and do the impossible.

It is God's will for me to live a fruitful life for His glory. His power flows to and through me. I believe it's God's will for me to be healed, prosperous, and free. All things in the will of God are possible for me because I believe in the Lord's goodness.

Big ideas come from forward-thinking people who challenge the norm, think outside the box, and invent the world they see inside rather than submitting to the limitations of current dilemmas.

BISHOP T.D. JAKES

PURPOSE AND DESTINY

BEING A GAME-CHANGER

The Bible is full of heroes of faith who went against the world's flow to do something great for God's glory. I think of the shepherd boy who killed a giant or the Pharisee who went from killing Christians to writing two-thirds of the New Testament.

When we encounter God and dare to believe Him at His Word, we are transformed into game-changers—people who cause dynamic shifts in the world around us and the lives of others. As you follow Jesus, He will cause you to think outside of norms and traditions to reveal something unique through you that this world has never seen.

He wants to impart wisdom to you, enhance your creativity, and use you to show others how they, too, can overcome and live out their purpose. There is something awesome inside of you that needs to get out. My prayer is that with the Spirit's help, everything God placed in you will be unleashed and cause a ripple effect unto the glory of God.

I walk in the wisdom of God. The Spirit of God enables me to live a supernatural life and go beyond my past limitations. I am anointed, creative, productive, and I add value everywhere I go. I am a vessel of God's game-changing power in Jesus' name.

"For I know the plans I have for you," declares the LORD, "plans to prosper you and not to harm you, plans to give you hope and a future."

JEREMIAH 29:11, NIV

PURPOSE AND DESTINY

A GOD PLAN

When we are uncertain of our future or the next steps we should take, we can take comfort in our connection to our strategic God. He made His plan for your life long before you were ever a baby in your mother's womb. He knows what He's placed in you and where He wants to use you for His glory.

You may be dealing with wounds from your past or facing present-day pressure. God's plan for you remains. Let these words comfort you as you look to your future through a different lens. God only has goodness to give you.

Far too many people wake up every day in despair because they don't have hope. They're facing lack, and they feel unprotected. When you're facing doubt or heaviness, remember that God's plan is to prosper you and protect you. He wants you to look toward the future with confident expectation of experiencing His unmerited favor. It's not too late. You haven't missed your destiny. God still has a good plan for you. Believe in His faithfulness to bring it to pass.

Thank You, Lord, for Your good plans for my life. Your will is better than mine because You know me better than I know myself. I reject the enemy's discouragement over my past and look forward to my future with confident expectation that You have made a way to prosper and protect my life.

And we know that all things work together for good to those who love God, to those who are the called according to *His* purpose.

ROMANS 8:28, NKJV

PURPOSE AND DESTINY

ALL THINGS WORKING FOR YOU

Nothing is ever perfect on this side of heaven. We suffer setbacks, disappointments, and trouble that stems from external sources as well as our own bad decisions. The beauty of this verse is that it shows God's omnipotent ability to turn even life's mess into a masterpiece.

Many times, we don't see how God can turn something bad into good while we are still going through adversity. It's only after the dust settles and our emotions calm that we see God was at work all along.

Some of my biggest mistakes were the catalysts for my biggest breakthroughs. No matter what you're facing right now, trust God to work it out for your good.

You have a love relationship with the Father. He has called you and anointed you with purpose. He knew every detour you would take before He determined your end. You haven't fallen so far that God can't get you back on track and turn drama into something beautiful.

Lord, I don't always understand everything about life, but You do. I believe You can turn my pain into something beautiful. You didn't say You'd make some things work for my good. You said ALL THINGS. I believe in Your goodness to produce a turnaround.

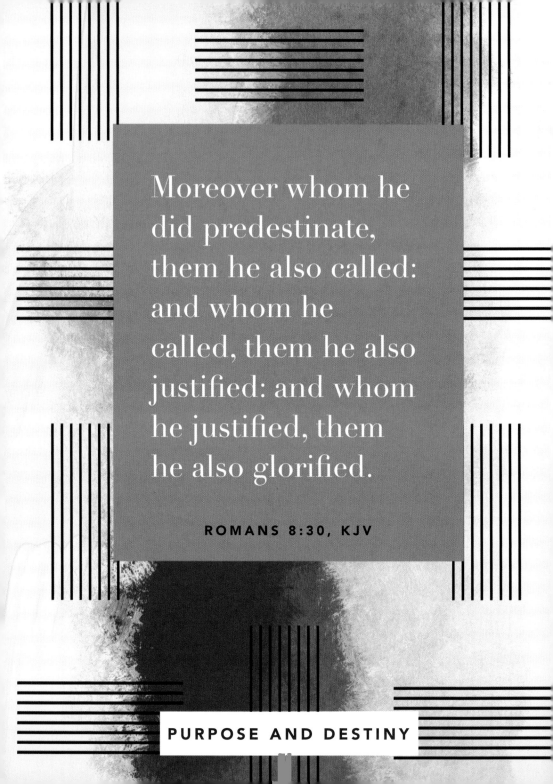

Moreover whom he did predestinate, them he also called: and whom he called, them he also justified: and whom he justified, them he also glorified.

ROMANS 8:30, KJV

PURPOSE AND DESTINY

15

DESTINED
FOR GLORY

Nothing about who you are is an afterthought with God. He knew you before you were born and planned your life's course. You've been predestined for His glory. He is calling out to you through the wisdom of His Word and the Holy Spirit, telling you of your new identity in Christ.

As a believer in Christ, you've been made righteous. Your path to glory begins with renewing your mind to this truth. Justification by the blood of Jesus is the launching pad into the blessings of God. He has made a promise to those He made righteous: He is going to show you His glory.

I love God's answer when Moses beseeched the Lord to show him His glory. God said, *"I will make all My goodness pass before you..."* (Exodus 33:19, NKJV).

As a justified child of God, you can expect to see the Lord's goodness. You may not be all you were created to be at this moment, but you are on your way. The Lord is with you, taking you to greater glory one step at a time.

Lord, I'm grateful that I was destined and called by You before the foundation of the world. I am justified as righteous by the blood of Jesus. I'm believing You to take me from faith to faith and glory to glory by Your grace. Amen.

Let your eyes look straight ahead, And your eyelids look right before you. Ponder the path of your feet, And let all your ways be established.

PROVERBS 4:25–26, NKJV

PURPOSE AND DESTINY

ESTABLISHED IN THE WAY

When we bring our minds and thoughts into focus, powerful things can happen. In fact, the ability to focus is one of God's gifts to mankind. I believe this verse is talking about seeing on two different planes—physical and spiritual.

Natural eyesight is a blessing because it gives us the ability to take in the beautiful world God created and guides us in everything we do in our daily life, from reading, eating, walking, driving, etc.

Beyond physical sight is the ability to see your world through God's eyes. This is called vision. When you can see and believe God's vision for your life with clear spiritual eyes on the inside, it will aid on the outside. You will begin to ponder your path and the decisions you make because you filter the world's external stimuli through the lens of your inner vision. When the enemy tries to draw you away, you won't be distracted from the established path God has for you.

My eyes look straight ahead to God's Word and His promises for my life. Holy Spirit, help me to turn away from lures and distractions. I declare the light of Your wisdom guides the path of my feet. Establish Your plans and purposes for my life in Jesus' name.

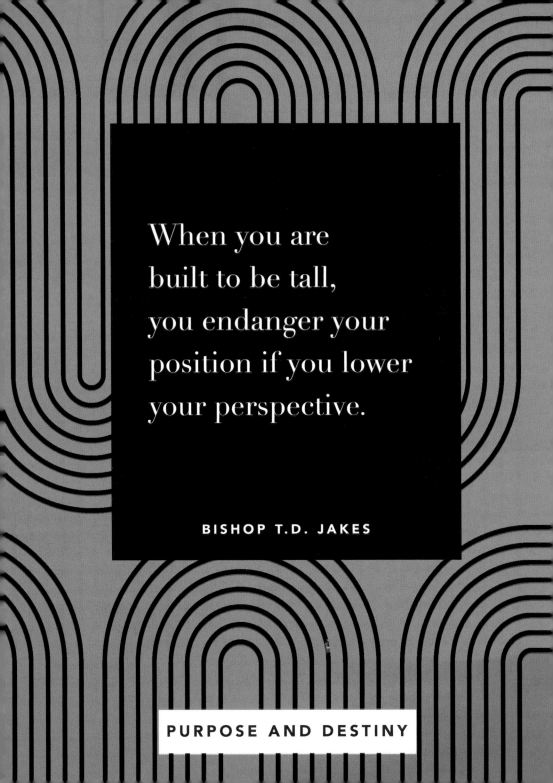

When you are
built to be tall,
you endanger your
position if you lower
your perspective.

BISHOP T.D. JAKES

PURPOSE AND DESTINY

ACCEPTING GREATNESS

Ephesians 2:6 says that God "...raised us up together, and made us sit together in heavenly places in Christ Jesus..." (NKJV). That's heaven's view of you as a born-again believer. Through your life's negative experiences, the enemy is going to do his best to convince you otherwise.

God didn't create us to be small, shrinking, insecure, and fearful. His Spirit is beckoning you to come up higher in how you see yourself and see your life. Don't allow the external evidence you see with your physical eyes to distract you from the truth. Facts can change, but the truth is eternal.

God's everlasting Word to you says that you are blessed with all spiritual blessings in heavenly places in Christ (Ephesians 1:3). Don't allow your haters to lower your vision to their level. Look to Jesus, and He will cause you to rise higher and higher!

I was made to express the excellencies of Jesus. I rebuke every lie of the enemy that would attempt to bring me down from my exalted status in Christ. I serve a big God, and I set my perspective and expectations on the One who never fails.

"... 'My counsel shall stand, And I will do all My pleasure' ... Indeed I have spoken *it*; I will also bring it to pass. I have purposed *it*; I will also do it."

ISAIAH 46:10-11, NKJV

PURPOSE AND DESTINY

HIS UNCHANGEABLE PURPOSE

When God comes up with a plan, He is His own counsel. He is all-knowing and needs no one's input. What He determines is best is what will stand for eternity. There are things God wants to do in your life that will bring Him pleasure. He intends to perform them. Before the foundation of the world, He created a way for you to be washed from sin and molded into the character of love. He spoke it, and it has come to pass through the sacrifice of Jesus.

Remember these truths when you're tempted to let life's inconveniences steal your joy or when your soul feels so heavy you can barely stand it. I do this in my own life. When we feel sadness settling on our souls, we must remember what God spoke over us and that it will come to pass. Our role is to believe what He said.

He's taking you somewhere good. Agree with His unchangeable purpose by speaking what He's said about you in faith as a habit.

Lord, I submit to Your plans and counsel. It is the only thing that is stable enough to stand for eternity. Do all You please in my life. Make your desire MY desire. Thank You for bringing to pass the things You have spoken to me through Your promises. Amen.

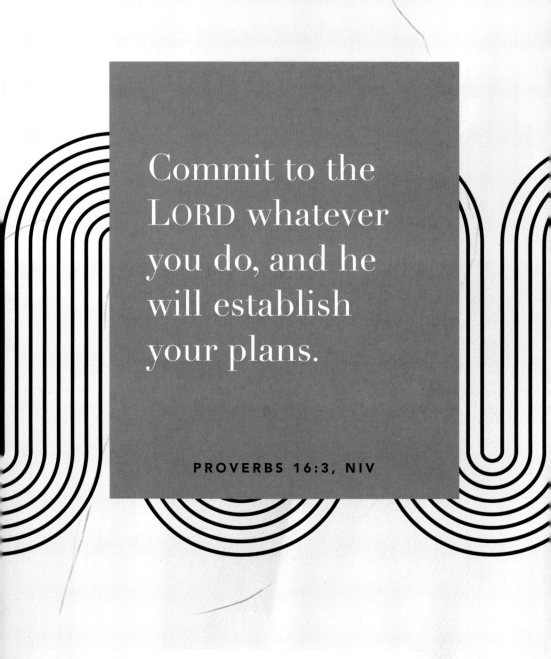

Commit to the LORD whatever you do, and he will establish your plans.

PROVERBS 16:3, NIV

PURPOSE AND DESTINY

ESTABLISHED BY GOD

God should be the primary motivation for everything we do. This is, however, not always the case because sometimes we allow the voice of the flesh to taint the reason why we do what we do. Sometimes we're motivated by things like money or another person's acceptance. Those things are too unstable. To build our lives on these things would cause instability.

We are meant to build our lives on the rock of God's approval. What has God given you that was intended to bless you and others? Don't fall for the enemy's trick. Take your plans, gifts, relationships, career, and everything else you are engaged in and commit them to the Lord. From a foundation of trust, He wants to establish your way into a true strategy that will cause you to arrive at your destination.

I commit my thoughts, ways, and plans to the Lord. I believe Him to establish and bring to pass the vision He has placed in my heart.

But you *are* a chosen generation, a royal priesthood, a holy nation, His own special people, that you may proclaim the praises of Him who called you out of darkness into His marvelous light; . . .

1 PETER 2:9, NKJV

PURPOSE AND DESTINY

YOUR ROYAL IDENTITY

When God chooses you, it reflects His desire and purpose for you. He has made your name synonymous with royalty and holiness. Some may scoff at that idea, thinking, *Me?! A holy priest? You should've seen what I was doing late last night.*

I understand. We don't always reflect God in our broken humanity. Yet, since Jesus died, you are still called to bear heaven's royal identity. God's repositioning strategy is to shift your mindset from the old way by revealing an understanding of who Jesus is and who you are in Him. As you mature in Him, others around you will begin to recognize that you've changed. You don't have the same triggers, insecurities, etc.

We bring praise to God as we thank Him for freeing us from our inner darkness day by day, year after year, for all eternity. What a glorious life you have been called to live in Jesus!

God chose me to live a royal life. I am made holy in Christ.
I am a special and unique individual whose life reflects
God's goodness and gives Him praise. I am free from the
darkness of sin by the light of Jesus Christ. Amen.

The fact that you yearn for more doesn't mean you're ungrateful for what you have or that you're greedy. It means you have a higher calling—the yearning inside calls to you.

BISHOP T.D. JAKES

PURPOSE AND DESTINY

ANSWERING THE CALL

Yearning for more is a sign we've heard the still, small voice of God, hearkening us to rise above fear and our comfort zones and step into greatness. I had a yearning on the inside of me to preach the gospel. The seed God planted in my heart was small. We just endeavored to remain faithful to where we started, which was in a basement with 12 elementary-age students and two volunteer teachers. I was only 18 years old myself!

When Serita and I started The Potter's House over 40 years ago, we aspired to do what we believed the Lord said. We didn't want to be prisoners of fear. So, my family packed up and launched out from the hills of West Virginia.

Serita and I prayed for pure motives and the Lord's strength for the Dallas transition. We had no idea thousands of people would join the church on the first day! We were just focused on answering the call.

As I reflect on 65 years, my main passion is to inspire you to answer the call of God's yearning in your heart.

I don't want to limit You, Lord. You came to give me life and life more abundantly. I'm grateful for all You've done for me. And I thank You for more expressions of Your goodness to come. I celebrate where You've brought me; while I rejoice in the expectation of where You're taking me.

Finally, brothers and sisters, whatever is true, whatever is noble, whatever is right, whatever is pure, whatever is lovely, whatever is admirable—if anything is excellent or praiseworthy—think about such things.

PHILIPPIANS 4:8, NIV

SOUL WELLNESS

22

AIM YOUR THOUGHTS

When a verse begins with "finally" in the Bible, it usually reflects a summation of a previous line of thought and discourse. It's the last thing the writer wants his audience to remember if they don't remember anything they read up to that point. It's the one nugget they want you to take away with you.

The one nugget the apostle Paul hoped the budding Philippian body of believers would grasp from his letter was this: Our lives go in the direction of our most dominant thoughts.

We've been given autonomy by God to choose our thoughts. It's up to us to choose well. When tempted, submit negative thinking to the Lord. Give Him an opportunity to mold and heal your heart in moments of pressure. Choose to think of what's lovely, kind, inspiring, brave, healing, and restoring . . . think of JESUS. As your thoughts begin to center on Him, your emotions, decisions, actions, habits, and even your personality will begin to reflect Christ.

God has given me the authority to choose what I think. I lift my mind to things of truth, nobility, righteousness, and love. I cast down the thoughts of the flesh and embrace praiseworthy inclinations.

For thou shalt eat the labour of thine hands: happy shalt thou be, and it shall be well with thee.

PSALM 128:2, KJV

SOUL WELLNESS

THE LABOR OF YOUR HANDS

Don't ignore what God places in your hands. What's in your hands has been invested with value because it came from a heavenly Source. Be like the apostle Paul, who said the Lord helped Him to labor more abundantly because of the grace of God that was with him (1 Corinthians 15:10).

Any person on this planet who chooses to work unto the Lord with the gifts he has been given will reap the benefits of multiplied fruitfulness. I can testify to the truth that something dynamic shifts when we engage in what we were born to do. The most immediate effect is that we begin to live happier lives, knowing we are working unto the Lord. He then enables us to enjoy the blessings that come as we work and succeed in our giftings.

Jesus wants your life to be well in every area as you enjoy His goodness. Encouraging ourselves in the Lord enables us to live this life free from being paralyzed in unproductivity by negative emotions. We are then free to do the very thing God gave us to do with no fear or guilt.

I am thankful for the work of my hands that the Lord has given me. I am skilled at what I do, and my gift commands attention in the marketplace. I profit well by the grace of God. I am happy in the Lord and all is well with me in Jesus' name.

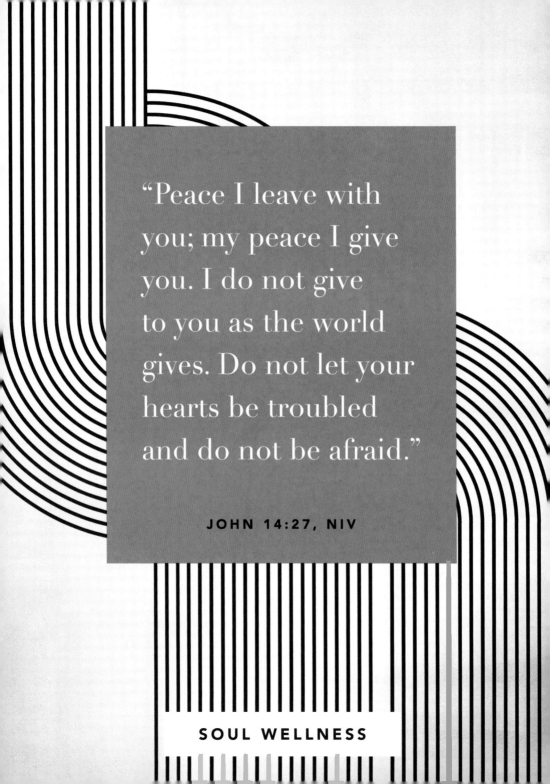

"Peace I leave with you; my peace I give you. I do not give to you as the world gives. Do not let your hearts be troubled and do not be afraid."

JOHN 14:27, NIV

SOUL WELLNESS

24

JESUS' PEACE

Jesus left you a gift when He ascended to heaven. He left you His peace. Not the false hope and substitute comfort the world offers. When trouble knocks on the door of our hearts with fear or despair, we can rest knowing Jesus is our peace.

We don't have to fear because He loves us and has forgiven our sins. Knowledge of guilt for wrongdoing is what causes people to tiptoe around God's throne instead of boldly drawing near in their time of need.

Don't let your heart be troubled. You are God's beloved. Go to Him in prayer and exchange your trouble for His peace. In Hebrew, the word peace is translated as shalom, meaning nothing is missing or broken.

Serita and I agree by faith with you that His grace will bring you out of trouble with nothing missing or broken.

I walk in the peace of Jesus Christ. The world gives false peace, hope, and rest. Jesus gives me His true peace as a gift. I rebuke fear in Jesus' name. Amen!

Like a city whose walls are broken through is a person who lacks self-control.

PROVERBS 25:28, NIV

SOUL WELLNESS

CONTROLLING YOUR EMOTIONS

When we don't allow our lives to be led by Spirit-directed boundaries, we are like a city that lacks defense. In Bible days, cities without walls were easily ransacked by invading armies. God doesn't want our lives to be vulnerable to the enemy's attacks.

The blessing He has placed inside of you by way of the Spirit is the fruit of self-control, which is a component of the love of God. Ultimately, it's the love of Christ that constrains or controls us. (2 Corinthians 5:18-19).

In these last days, I believe God wants to fortify your defense and offense through the power of love. Go to God in prayer and ask Him to help you put Holy Ghost fences around the precious things in your life that He has given you.

Through the help of the Holy Spirit, I bear the fruit of self-control in my life. Boundaries and restraint are necessary for successful spiritual, relational, mental, and physical living. I respond to life in the Lord's wisdom and come away from hasty, fleshy tendencies.

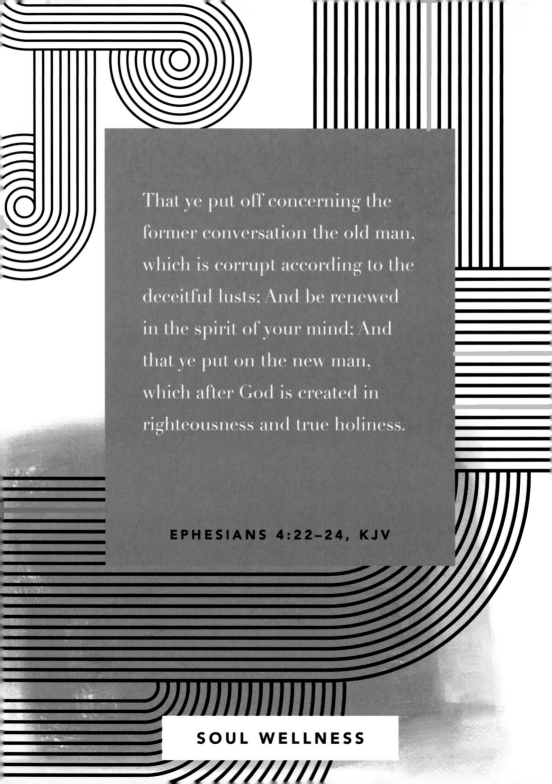

That ye put off concerning the former conversation the old man, which is corrupt according to the deceitful lusts; And be renewed in the spirit of your mind; And that ye put on the new man, which after God is created in righteousness and true holiness.

EPHESIANS 4:22–24, KJV

SOUL WELLNESS

26

FREEDOM FROM DECEITFUL LUST

I find it interesting that the Greek word for conversation in this verse means manner of life, conduct, or behavior. God is showing us that wherever our words go, our lives will follow. When we think and speak about ourselves in line with the old way, we produce fruit that is inconsistent with the Spirit inside of us.

The old way of living was corrupt because we couldn't see that we were being deceived by the flesh's appetites. Now, because of Jesus, we can have our minds reframed by His Word.

When Paul talks about the "spirit of the mind," he is talking about the deepest level—our subconscious mind. This is the place where our knee-jerk responses originate. God wants to impact your mind at the deepest level with His Word to point out that it affects your automatic responses. When our subconscious mind is renewed, our automatic responses will tend to lean toward love rather than the flesh.

I put off the old way of thinking and living that dominated my old man. I am renewed in the deepest parts of my soul through my relationship with Christ. His Word and Spirit help me to escape the deceitful lusts of this world. Amen.

Too many people want the appearance of winning rather than the practice and hard work that create a true champion.

BISHOP T.D. JAKES

SOUL WELLNESS

27

SELF-MASTERY

I can't tell you how many times I've preached to empty chairs since God launched me into ministry over 40 years ago. When we first started the church, I remember times when no one showed up. I still preached with everything God gave me.

In retrospect, I can look back and see how God was building, sharpening, and crafting me. By the time the large crowds started showing up, I was prepared. The full stadium didn't get a different T.D. Jakes than the empty room. I was the same me because God already showed me who I was during my season of obscurity.

Take the time to allow God to help you develop championship-level routines and habits. Keep your motives pure. Only endeavor to work pleasingly unto the Lord, trusting that your time and labor of love in His service will be rewarded. The true prize is when God shows you the significance of who you were created to be.

Lord, You said that success and wealth obtained through haste are vain. Help me to develop the character of Christ so that I may please You at all times, even behind closed doors. Help me to develop a way of thinking and a routine for success. I'm a champion in Christ.

Let all bitterness, and wrath, and anger, and clamour, and evil speaking, be put away from you, with all malice: and be ye kind one to another, tenderhearted, forgiving one another, even as God for Christ's sake hath forgiven you.

EPHESIANS 4:31–32, KJV

SOUL WELLNESS

28

EMOTIONS AND RELATIONSHIPS

So many people lose God-ordained relationships that could have been a blessing to them because of careless words and actions. The Bible doesn't say to forsake some bitterness or ungodly anger but to let it all go. When we speak in line with the world instead of the Spirit, we are not only harming ourselves; we are impacting the people around us as well.

Our words and actions matter. Ten spies came back from the promised land with a negative report and caused a whole generation of people to miss out on God's blessing (Numbers 13:32–33).

Ask the Lord to help you cultivate words and actions that pour kindness and encouragement into others' lives. Sow forgiveness to people who hurt you. As a believer in Christ, this verse places God's forgiveness of your sins in the past tense. Since He has already decided to forgive ALL your sin, extend the same forgiveness to the lives of others. God wants to move you beyond the hurt, rejection, betrayal, and lies they told. Get on with your life and watch God turn it around for your good.

I bear the fruit of love by the power of the Holy Spirit. I walk like Christ and reject all thoughts and feelings of bitterness, anger, jealousy, and gossip. I release kindness into my relationships and forgive others' faults as God has forgiven me in Jesus.

This book of the law shall not depart out of thy mouth; but thou shalt meditate therein day and night . . . for then thou shalt make thy way prosperous, and then thou shalt have good success.

JOSHUA 1:8, KJV

SOUL WELLNESS

29

MEDITATING ON THE WORD

Keeping our mouths full of God's Word is one of the most practical applications of our faith and trust in Him. It means something to heaven when you speak forth the rain of God even when your circumstances look barren as the desert.

When we speak and ponder God's Word throughout the day, our souls—mind, will, and emotions—are edified. Meditating on the Word produces answers, direction, and purpose. Meditating on the problem produces fear.

If we want our lives to be marked by the good success God has destined us for, let's become proactive in taking a few moments throughout our days to vocalize God's promises. It doesn't have to be anything deep or dramatic. Just open your mouth once a day and say, "Jesus loves me" out loud as a wise act of faith that all of heaven endorses.

Lord, help me to take time to meditate on Your Word daily. I speak forth Your Word. What You said about my life is true, and I add my agreement. Meditating on You produces wisdom for my good success.

The law of the LORD is perfect, refreshing the soul. The statutes of the LORD are trustworthy, making wise the simple.

PSALM 19:7, NIV

SOUL WELLNESS

30

A REFRESHED SOUL

With our collective screen time, to-do lists, binges, and isolation increasing, people need refreshment for their souls seemingly more than ever in the modern era. Some will turn to God to make sense of it all, and some won't. We get to choose to what or with whom we connect.

The shifting social norms and secular humanism provide no stability as public consensus switches with the passing decades. But one thing has stood the test of time: the Word of God. Jesus has spoken and continues to speak what will refresh your soul.

When our souls are watered with God's Word, it washes the dryness of negative emotions away, imparts wisdom for strategic living, and helps us line up our decision-maker with God's will.

God is trustworthy. What He speaks stands for eternity. The wisdom of His statutes cries aloud in the streets. Anyone lacking know-how can partake. The more we drink from God's well, the more we understand and the more at rest we become.

Lord, I embrace Your eternal Word in its fullness. Your promises uplift and refresh my soul—my mind, will, and emotions. Your principles and ways can be trusted and make me supernaturally smarter in areas where I need to develop.

Be ye angry, and sin not: let not the sun go down upon your wrath: Neither give place to the devil.

EPHESIANS 4:26–27, KJV

SOUL WELLNESS

31

NO PLACE IN YOU

Some people think the Bible forbids anger. Anger, in and of itself, is not a sin. In fact, sometimes anger may be encouraged if it's for the sake of something righteous and holy. That kind of anger should be acted on while it can be used for something good. This could be the person who is fed up with falling into the same pattern and gets angry enough to make a change. We want to act before this kind of passionate motivation burns out. Do it while the sun is high in the sky. Not acting on this kind of anger is a sin.

From another perspective, holding on to anger motivated by selfishness instead of forgiveness enables the enemy to affect our minds and relationships. Many a home has been dismantled because of an insensitive word or action out of selfish anger.

Ask the Lord to help you discern your anger. In moments of high emotion, we must learn to pause and give the Spirit time to speak. If our anger is motivated by holiness, He will give us the grace to act boldly. If it is motivated by the flesh, He can help us decipher and process the why behind what we're feeling.

Lord, I thank You that my anger is sanctified in Jesus. Let my anger be born out of righteousness and holiness, not selfish anger that is destructive to myself and others. The fruit of love governs my relationships, and I give no place to the flesh's selfishness.

He maketh me to lie
down in green pastures:
he leadeth me beside
the still waters. He
restoreth my soul: he
leadeth me in the paths
of righteousness for his
name's sake.

PSALM 23:2–3, KJV

SOUL WELLNESS

32

A RESTORED SOUL

I did some fascinating reading on sheep and shepherds. One of the things I learned is that sheep are not strong enough on their own to handle powerful currents of water. Rushing water, combined with the weight of their wool, will cause sheep to drown. It's the shepherd who guides the sheep to still waters where they can safely drink.

God is like that with us. He wants to lead us to good destinations. In a spiritual sense, our still waters are the times we spend fellowshipping with God in the Word, prayer, praise, etc. The more time we spend focused on Him, the more our souls are restored.

As He leads you in the knowledge of His righteousness, your life is transformed. Follow the rhythm of the Spirit. Allow the Great Shepherd to lead you through doors no man can open or shut!

The Lord helps me not internalize the stress and drama of modern living. My mind and emotions are at ease as my thoughts center on His promises. I drink from His presence, and I am refreshed and restored. He leads me in the righteousness of Christ. Amen.

Sometimes the hardest times in our lives do more to strengthen us than all our mountaintop experiences. Your success is imminent!

BISHOP T.D. JAKES

THE LORD'S DELIVERANCE

33

STRENGTHENED IN THE VALLEY

Life has its peaks and valleys. Sometimes we ride high on the waves of success. Other seasons are not so good, and some can be downright brutal. The Bible advises us to be joyful in the day of prosperity but to consider in the day of adversity (Ecclesiastes 7:14).

When we're experiencing the thrill of God's blessings, we should rejoice and praise Jesus for His bountiful abundance. Yet, life is not just about avoiding hard times. Dark days can teach you some of your most valuable lessons.

I remember when I lost my job, and everything we owned was at risk. With a young family to support, it was the darkest period of my life. Yet, this was when I received some of my most valued impartations from the Lord.

At a time when I was near to losing my mind because the stress was so great, God showed me He was faithful. Step by step, He took our family from losing everything to overflowing provision.

Praise God for His lessons in the storm and His goodness in the sunshine.

Lord, I thank You that failure and trying times are not the totality of my life's story. Help me to see every season, whether good or bad, through Your eyes. Help me to learn the lessons You are trying to show me in the prosperous and lean times. I succeed because of Christ.

The righteous cry out, and the LORD hears, And delivers them out of all their troubles. The LORD *is* near to those who have a broken heart, And saves such as have a contrite spirit. Many *are* the afflictions of the righteous, But the LORD delivers him out of them all.

PSALM 34:17–19, NKJV

THE LORD'S DELIVERANCE

34

HE HEARS YOU

Your faith paradigm shifts when you have confidence that God hears your cry. This passage mentions the word righteous not once but twice. Today, David is speaking to us through a praise song he wrote centuries ago.

It's true. You're going to have many afflictions in this life. Jesus promised us trouble-free living in heaven, not on earth. We can take comfort in knowing we can draw near to God's throne as the righteousness of God. There is no trouble you will encounter in this life for which He hasn't already preplanned a victory.

Take comfort in Jesus' words from Luke 18:7–8: "*And shall not God avenge his own elect, which cry day and night unto him, though he bear long with them? I tell you that he will avenge them speedily . . .*" (KJV). Speedily. I like that word. Come, quickly Lord. Amen.

Thank You, Lord, for hearing all my prayers, even the ones I didn't give voice to; you heard the cry of my heart. You deliver me from all my tests and trials. I am the righteousness of God and overcome every affliction in Jesus' name.

No temptation has overtaken you except such as is common to man; but God *is* faithful, who will not allow you to be tempted beyond what you are able, but with the temptation will also make the way of escape, that you may be able to bear *it*.

1 CORINTHIANS 10:13, NKJV

THE LORD'S DELIVERANCE

35

THE WAY OF ESCAPE

Ever since the fall in the garden of Eden, temptation has been a part of this life on earth. When we're going through tough times, sometimes we're tempted with self-pity, thinking we're the only ones. We're not. It's all common to the human condition.

We should be thankful that the light of God's faithfulness cuts through the fog of temptation that tries to blind us to God's goodness. He knows what you're going through isn't easy, but you are able to overcome in Him.

For every sinful pull, God provides a backdoor of escape. In moments when you want to yield to sin, the Spirit is speaking. Learn to pause. Hear Him. There is no trouble you may go through that Jesus has not already prepared a way of escape for you in advance. Hearken to His direction. Amen.

Thank You for being faithful to me in moments of temptation. If I am being tempted, it means I can resist in the strength of the Lord. You don't allow any temptation to come against me that's beyond my ability to resist. I receive Your way of escape.

So I say, walk by the Spirit, and you will not gratify the desires of the flesh.

GALATIANS 5:16, NIV

THE LORD'S DELIVERANCE

36

WALKING IN THE SPIRIT

I think sometimes people get confused when they see the word "flesh" in the Bible. Sometimes it refers to our physical body. Other times, it refers to our old way of thinking and emotions that can motivate the impulses of the body.

The old mindset—the flesh—has desires. Its desires are the opposite of the desires of your born-again spirit, where the Holy Spirit lives and wants to lead and guide you. The key is to be proactive in your relationship with Him.

This verse doesn't say to stop walking in the flesh and doing sinful things so you can walk in the Spirit. It says to engage the Spirit first, and you won't get caught up in the things the flesh desires.

As you focus on walking with the Lord and developing a personal relationship with Him, He will shape the desires of your heart. This approach puts the relationship first rather than our efforts to change ourselves.

I understand life has two choices: to walk guided by the Spirit or by carnal, old ways of thinking. Lord, help me to be proactive in thinking, speaking, and acting in sync with the desires of my born-again spirit. I make no provisions for indulging selfish lust in Jesus' name.

I can do all things through Christ who strengthens me.

PHILIPPIANS 4:13, NJKV

THE LORD'S DELIVERANCE

37

CHRIST'S STRENGTH

You were created to live in the anointing—the power of God. He wants to pour out His supernatural ability on you to cause you to do what you couldn't have done in your own natural ability.

Something powerful happens when the world sees the children of God walking in their purpose. When the church moves beyond singing and sermons and connects to the power of God, a tsunami of God's goodness will send ripples across the globe.

In these last days, all of creation is crying out in longing for the manifestation of those walking in the spiritual authority and power of the Lord (Romans 8:22). As the church rises up, the world will be drawn to our light as the power of God flows to and through us, pushing back darkness across the land!

The anointing of Jesus Christ empowers me to do everything I need to do in this life. I am infused with inner strength by the Holy Spirit. I face all obstacles in God's might, not my own.

Put on the whole armour of God, that ye may be able to stand against the wiles of the devil. For we wrestle not against flesh and blood, but against principalities, against powers, against the rulers of the darkness of this world, against spiritual wickedness in high places.

EPHESIANS 6:11–12, KJV

THE LORD'S DELIVERANCE

38

THE ARMOR OF GOD

God has given you weapons to use in the battles of life. The enemy is going to come against your mind every day with his darts—thoughts rooted in fear that are contrary to God's promises for your life.

God provided armor for the war in your mind. He wants to empower you to be able to stand in the day of adversity. His armor is the truth about who you are in Jesus; when the enemy shows up with thoughts that devalue you, fire back with Scripture about your worth in Christ.

Even in our daily interactions, we must remember that our fight is never against people. We are opposed by demonic spirits and influences. We've been given spiritual authority as the righteousness of God to deal with them. Jesus already defeated the devil on the cross, making an open show of him. Our job is to use the tools He gave us to continue to walk the road He has already paved for us.

I put on the whole armor of God, which are the promises of God in the Word spoken over my life. He forgave me and made me righteous. This enables me to stand against the enemy's schemes to torture me with guilt, shame, and condemnation. I take authority over every demonic force in Jesus' name.

Never try to make sense of your trial while you're in it. Focus on surviving it, not understanding it.

BISHOP T.D. JAKES

THE LORD'S DELIVERANCE

39

SURVIVING AND THRIVING

Some things Serita and I went through times in our lives that were so tough that trying to figure out all the whys behind what we were dealing with was counterproductive. It took enough just to believe God to come out of our drama without adding extra pressure.

When the pressure of life is heavy, don't overload yourself with the extra task of trying to understand things you don't need to know in the current season. Trust that God will reveal all things in due time.

He wants to help you and not lay a burden on you. When you're walking through the valley of the shadow of death, the only thing you need to focus on is Jesus being with you and His love for you. Anything else will cause your mind to be overworked. God's got your back. Trust Him to give you all the understanding and closure you need at the right time.

Lord, help me to understand that I don't need to understand everything, especially when I'm going through a hard time. Instead, I choose to focus on Your faithfulness and how good You are to me.

"Have I not commanded you? Be strong and of good courage; do not be afraid, nor be dismayed, for the LORD your God *is* with you wherever you go."

JOSHUA 1:9, NKJV

THE LORD'S DELIVERANCE

40

HE'S WITH YOU

The Lord spoke these words to Joshua after Moses was dead. Imagine how he felt. The man leading millions of Israelites in the desert that he had served under and learned from was no longer around. Now, he was responsible for leading the people.

Being fearful that we might not be ready for a particular task is a normal human reaction. Joshua had a choice. He could have shrunk back after Moses died, but if he had, he would have missed the promised land. The key to embracing such a huge undertaking is to know that God is with you.

Jesus said He'd never leave us or forsake us (Hebrews 13:5). Take courage knowing that you aren't facing your challenge alone. God's guaranteed presence will shift things in your favor.

Serita and I are praying that you come to know the intimacy of the Lord's presence and the favor of His perfectly timed help in the seasons you need Him most. Amen.

Lord, I stand against the fear that is rampant in the world. I am Your child and loved by You, which means there is nothing for me to fear. When fear knocks on the door of my soul, help me to move forward by Your grace.

LORD my God, I take refuge in you; save and deliver me from all who pursue me.

PSALM 7:1, NIV

THE LORD'S DELIVERANCE

41

YOUR REFUGE

Refuge is defined as the condition of being safe or sheltered from pursuit, danger, or trouble. This is what the Lord is to us. Jesus said the storms of life would come (Matthew 7:25). We are all pursued by different things at different times in our lives. Some are being pursued by depression. Others need refuge from physical sickness. No matter what we are facing, God has already provided the prescription before our trouble shows up.

Notice this is not a passive thing. David said he took refuge in the Lord. He decided to take advantage of what God was offering. Take your refuge. Jesus is your deliverer. Don't let anything or anyone keep you from claiming your position in God's shelter.

If you are facing a storm in your life right now, Serita and I pray for the comfort, direction, and favor of the Holy Spirit on you and your entire family in Jesus' name.

Lord, when negativity bombards my soul, I run to You. If fear, sickness, lack, hurt, or any other device of the enemy should pursue me, I believe Your deliverance will be seen in my life. Amen.

Be sober, be vigilant; because your adversary the devil walks about like a roaring lion, seeking whom he may devour. Resist him, steadfast in the faith, knowing that the same sufferings are experienced by your brotherhood in the world.

1 PETER 5:8–9, NKJV

THE LORD'S DELIVERANCE

42

EXPOSING THE IMPOSTER

One time I heard someone say, "The shadow of a lion ain't never bite anybody!" That got me thinking. The Bible didn't say the devil was a lion. It said he walks around like a lion. Jesus is the only real lion depicted in Scripture. The enemy is a total imposter!

To see through his scheme, we must be clear and self-controlled in our thinking. The enemy wants us to think he can just devour anybody, but he can't. He only has access to those who don't know how to resist him by faith.

Take comfort that you're not in this fight alone. Believers around the globe are engaged in some form of resistance against the enemy's mind games. The way to win is by arming yourself against his lies with the truths of God's Word. Counteract his lie with a promise that fits your specific situation, and tell him to flee in the name of Jesus!

I am submitted to God and God alone. I can resist the enemy, and he has to flee from me. I belong to Jesus, and the enemy has no hold, right, or authority in my life. I am free in Jesus' name!

Those who belong to Christ Jesus have crucified the flesh with its passions and desires.

GALATIANS 5:24, NIV

THE LORD'S DELIVERANCE

43

THE FLESH CRUCIFIED

As born-again believers, we are Christ's special possession. We belong to Him. This blessed position endows us with benefits we would never see outside of our relationship with Jesus. This fascinating verse has an interesting meaning in the past tense form.

Notice, it doesn't say those who are in Christ will crucify or overcome the flesh. It says they have already done it. According to God's perspective, we've already died to the desires and passions of the flesh.

Life changes when you learn to see through a spiritual lens. In the natural, we are always faced with lying evidence and symptoms of an old problem that Jesus has already solved. We may not have fully matured into our stature in Christ, but according to the New Testament, we have already died to sin and are now alive in Christ (Romans 6:11). So, be patient with your broken humanity. God is growing you up in the character of Jesus Christ step by step.

I belong to Jesus, and I have died to the old way of thinking and living because I've been crucified with Christ. My relationship with the Holy Spirit births holy desires in my life.

My mother would take the Band-Aid off, clean the wound, and say, "Things that are covered don't heal well." Mother was right. Things that are covered don't heal well.

BISHOP T.D. JAKES

HEALTH AND HEALING

44

UNCOVER
THE WOUND

Sometimes when we're hurt, we are so shocked at what's happening that our only response is to bottle it up and bury how much it affects us. We brush it off, quote a Scripture, and move on. The problem is, the hurt we didn't deal with will one day start dealing with us.

God wants us to know His truth in our inward parts. He wants you to be truthful with Him about your pain so you can receive His healing. The soothing balm of the Spirit is always available to you, but He's a gentleman. He won't force Himself into an area where you won't invite Him.

Invite God into the hurt you've suffered. Pray and ask Him to shine His light on anything you may have buried that hasn't fully healed. He wants you whole on the inside so you can be a blessing to others around you. Healed people are God's best advertising platform for salvation. Let Him use you by uncovering the wound.

Lord, You said You desire truth in my inward parts. I uncover and bring my pain and shame to You. I shove the darkness in my life into the light of Your Word, and I am healed!

The LORD is close to the brokenhearted and saves those who are crushed in spirit.

PSALM 34:18, NIV

HEALTH AND HEALING

45

HEALING FOR A BROKEN HEART

When our hearts are broken, the Lord wants us to know that proximity to Him matters. Our feelings try to tell us that God is a million miles away when we're in pain. He's not. In fact, He is close to the brokenhearted and saves those who are crushed in spirit.

Jesus' ears are tuned in to your pain. His saving credentials go beyond your initial born-again experience. He is your Savior for eternity. He never tires of you and is interceding on your behalf in heaven. Your crushing is not your end. Take courage. There is healing for your broken heart at the throne of God's grace.

God used the nights I cried myself to sleep to develop me into the person I am today. I believe He is doing the same for you. Trust Him to use your crushing as the launchpad into your destiny in Him.

Lord, when my heart breaks, help me to know how close You are to me. Manifest Your love in a way that I'll recognize Your tailor-made approach and awareness of me. You lift my wounded soul.

O God, thou art my God; early will I seek thee: my soul thirsteth for thee, my flesh longeth for thee in a dry and thirsty land, where no water is.

PSALM 63:1, KJV

HEALTH AND HEALING

46

HEALING FOR A DRY SOUL

King David's words in this Psalm sound like they came from a man who has come to the end of a long journey. He'd tried every substitute for God, and his soul's hunger and thirst remained. But in God, David finally located his truest desire.

The spiritual bond we have with God is inescapable. Nothing in the created world will ever be able to take His place. Our futile search for drinking water from the world's fountain always keeps us thirsty for more. Our increasing unfulfillment is meant to drive us to our knees before the Lord.

Your search in the desert for an oasis has come to an end. Let God's Word water the garden of your soul. I promise you, something beautiful will grow. Ultimately, the more whole your soul becomes, the more God will begin to use you to uplift others who are stuck in the same ditch where you once found yourself. Praise God!

Help me to understand that You alone quench my soul's thirst. I acknowledge my need for You, Lord. My entire being longs for You. As I drink from Your goodness, I am satisfied.

Have mercy upon me, O LORD; for I am weak: O LORD, heal me; for my bones are vexed.

PSALM 6:2, KJV

HEALTH AND HEALING

47

HEALING FOR THE WEAK

God's mercy is infused into our lives in both noticeable and subtle ways. We won't know all the times His mercy kept bad things from us until we get to heaven. Mercy is one of God's calling cards—a distinguishing characteristic of His inherent nature.

When you are weak, where do you turn? Is it to God, or someone, or something else? The Holy Spirit is present to help and heal you. When you feel sapped of strength in your body, call on Him. He is in you to quicken your body (Romans 8:11).

One of the things that keep us from receiving God's help is that we don't go to Him as our first option. We wait until the faulty sources in our comfort zones fail us. Then we rush to God in a frenzy for a miracle.

Even in this position, God is still not angry or disappointed in us. He just doesn't want us to be behind the eight ball. Go to Him before trouble even shows up. He's willing to show you His strength.

Thank You, Father, that there is mercy for my weaknesses. When my soul and body are weary, You empower me with Your loving touch. Amen.

Heal me, LORD, and I will be healed; save me and I will be saved, for you are the one I praise.

JEREMIAH 17:14, NIV

HEALTH AND HEALING

48

YOUR SAVIOR

I like how this verse reflects two different positions on each side of the two "ands." In both cases, we see a request being made and then followed up with an admission of certainty that the request will be granted.

This kind of confident expression can only come out of a heart that is sure of its relationship with God. A heart that believes in the One to whom the request is being made and in His ability to do something about it.

A heart that rests assured it can receive from God is forged in the fires of intimate relationship. Over time, day-to-day interaction produces trust. That trust produces rest, which opens the door to your breakthrough. Believe you receive in Jesus' name!

God is the One you praise because He is the only One who can make the difference in your life. Be fearless and repeat back to God, in faith, exactly what you expect Him to do based on what He promised you!

My deepest needs can only be met by Jesus. If I need healing, He is my healer. If I need to be rescued, He is my deliverer. I praise Him because He is my everything.

. . . You restored me to health and let me live. Surely it was for my benefit that I suffered such anguish. In your love you kept me from the pit of destruction; you have put all my sins behind your back.

ISAIAH 38:16–17, NIV

HEALTH AND HEALING

49

BEHIND HIS BACK

This verse ends with an interesting punchline to which I want you to pay attention. It says He put your sins behind His back. I wondered why God would mention that in connection to healing? The Lord showed me the context.

These are the words of a person who knows their suffering has been caused by their own foolish decisions. They recognized it was a benefit for them to learn from the consequences of taking a wrong turn, just as God had warned them.

Despite that, God's goodness is the hero of this verse. He still saves us from our consequences, even though we caused them with our disobedience. Why? Because He can't see your sins. They're behind His back. He is just looking at how much He loves you!

Father, thank You for restoring my health and making it better than it was before. In Your love, You forgot my sins, healed me, and saved me from destruction. Thank You, Jesus.

One of the great
healing balms of
the Holy Spirit
is forgiveness. To
forgive is to break
the link between you
and your past.

BISHOP T.D. JAKES

HEALTH AND HEALING

50

HEAVEN'S HEALING BALM

Some God-ordained relationships go stale because forgiveness isn't dispersed in regular doses. Just like a garden or lawn that needs to be watered on a regular basis to avoid dryness, kindness and forgiveness keep the love in our homes from withering.

Serita and I have practiced forgiveness in our marriage for decades. Over the years, I found I had issues with the very thing I was judging her for in one way or another. I believe humility is our ally in our quest for loving relationships and breaking our link to each other's past offenses.

On your journey of health and wholeness, remember to take a healthy dose of forgiveness for yourself as well. Get rid of the weight and sin of your past, so you can run the race God has for you (Hebrews 12:1).

I declare I receive the Lord's forgiveness through the blood of Jesus. I am healed from my past. I am now free to enjoy my present days to the fullest while I look forward with hope to the Lord's future goodness.

"Nevertheless, I will bring health and healing to it; I will heal my people and will let them enjoy abundant peace and security."

JEREMIAH 33:6, NIV

HEALTH AND HEALING

51

GOD'S NEVERTHELESS

When we've experienced setbacks, and it appears our relief is far off, we need to tune our spiritual ears to God's "nevertheless." In the English language, this is a phrase we use when we are about to say something that contrasts what we just said.

In Scripture, God is usually on the other side of nevertheless. You may need healing or deliverance. You may have suffered a season of constricted circumstances. Heaven is saying even though you've been through it . . . NEVERTHELESS . . .

God always has a "nevertheless" on reserve for you. He is bringing peace and healing to you. Adjust your expectation to enjoy His abundant peace, protection, and provision.

Father, thank You for Your "nevertheless" in my life. No matter what has happened, Your abundant healing, peace, and security will be seen in my life because You love me.

And God shall wipe away all tears from their eyes; and there shall be no more death, neither sorrow, nor crying, neither shall there be any more pain: for the former things are passed away.

REVELATION 21:4, KJV

HEALTH AND HEALING

52

NO MORE TEARS

The future promise of heaven is not a pie-in-the-sky fairytale. It is our encouraging, great hope. We should look forward to it with expectation while still endeavoring to maximize everything God has given us access to while we're here on earth.

Sometimes, to rise above the pettiness of life, we must set our sights on a higher vision. Why give into foolish road rage in traffic when you are ultimately headed to heaven? Is the small thing we're upset about now going to matter in eternity? No.

God has seen the frustrations you've suffered on earth. He has a count in heaven of every tear you shed on Earth. He has special things planned for you when you arrive to meet Him. You will be blessed with things that delight you and are crafted to fit you like the finest tailor-made suit.

The former things—the shame of your youth, your pain, and even the ultimate enemy of death—are passing away. Praise Jesus!

I am grateful to look forward to the future promise of heaven. There will be no sickness, tears, or death. This truth gives me hope to live an overcoming life while here on Earth. Amen.

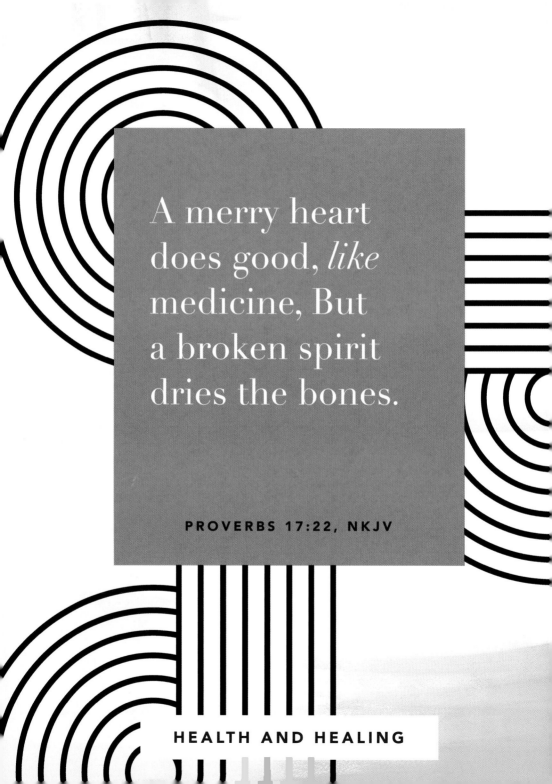

A merry heart does good, *like* medicine, But a broken spirit dries the bones.

PROVERBS 17:22, NKJV

HEALTH AND HEALING

53

BE MERRY

Some church folks are so serious they don't even know how to enjoy life. Some of the dysfunction in our souls is a result of simply taking life too seriously and not knowing how to be merry and have a good laugh.

We can become so uptight in our religiosity that we miss the simple pleasures of life that God meant for us to enjoy. No wonder the world has largely been turned off by our sour faces and sanctimonious displays.

Let's learn to have fun with God. Let's play, dance, and sing. So many people feel old because they bury their childlike feelings of simplicity, trust, and enjoyment in life that God gave them.

I'm giving you a homework assignment. Go find a funny book to read and laugh before the Lord, by faith, as if you don't have a care in the world! Heaven will smile, and hell will be totally confused! Your physical body will also benefit from the endorphins a little humor will release.

Lord, help me to find joy in life and have some fun. Help me not be so religious that I don't find opportunities to live and laugh. May your joy lift me and produce health in my body.

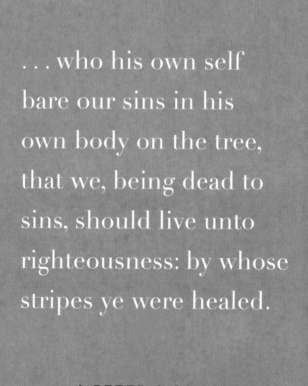

... who his own self bare our sins in his own body on the tree, that we, being dead to sins, should live unto righteousness: by whose stripes ye were healed.

1 PETER 2:24, KJV

HEALTH AND HEALING

54

CURSED ON THE TREE

Jesus was cursed when He hung on the tree. It was for a purpose—someone needed to bear our sins. The load was too heavy for us. So, He allowed Himself to be beaten and even hung on a cross. As a result, we went from being dead in sin to being dead TO sin. Which means our core nature has changed.

Now, with the Holy Spirit inside of us, we can live out our righteous identity in Christ. This is the foundation that causes God's healing power to flow in our lives. He took our sins in His body so we could receive His perfect health in our bodies.

Once again, this is another verse that positions the blessing of God in the past tense. Your healing has already happened in the spirit realm. Jesus' eternal payment gives you access to a perpetual waterfall of healing power.

Jesus, You bore the curse for me when You hung on the cross as me. Thank You that, through You, I have now died to sin and am free to live in righteousness. Your suffering 2,000 years ago produced my healing today. Amen.

He gives power
to the weak,
And to *those who
have* no might
He increases
strength.

ISAIAH 40:29, NKJV

HEALTH AND HEALING

55

THE INCREASER

God specializes in increasing things that appear small or insignificant upon first appearance. He loves to reveal Himself to the weary soul as the Increaser—One who builds up from a low state of being.

The key is that we must recognize we've come to the end of our own strength. If we think we have the power to change our situation without submitting to the Lord's help, we will continue to struggle.

When we come up under the eagle's wings of humility and admit we have no strength apart from God, we are lifted and able to fly above the storm's turbulence.

May you experience an increase in strength and vision for the season ahead. May God's touch turn your pain points into your greatest reasons to praise Him.

I believe the Lord's strength increases in me even when I feel like I can't go on any longer. He empowers me to keep living by lifting my soul out of the pit of despair and infusing might into my body.

Forgiveness
is about
empowering
yourself rather
than empowering
your past.

BISHOP T.D. JAKES

HEALTH AND HEALING

56

EMPOWERED BEYOND YOUR PAST

We will never be able to embrace our future until we allow forgiveness to adjust our perspective on our past. When we still see ourselves as unchanged and tied to what was, we enter destructive, repetitious cycles.

Many times, people are free, but their wrong mindset drives them back into bondage. Think about it. The children of Israel had been enslaved in Egypt for centuries and were willing to go back.

Unforgiveness is like that. It causes us to return to dead monuments of failure. God doesn't want you offering sacrifices on the altar of your past shame. He wants to empower you to walk into your future and move you beyond mourning over who you were and what you did.

Lord, You forgave me of all my sin because of the shed blood of Jesus. I receive Your forgiveness for my past sins. I am free to embrace the good future You have for me, Jesus. Amen.

Thou preparest a table before me in the presence of mine enemies: thou anointest my head with oil; my cup runneth over. Surely goodness and mercy shall follow me all the days of my life: and I will dwell in the house of the LORD for ever.

PSALM 23:5–6, KJV

PROVISION AND FULFILLMENT

57

FEASTING AT HIS TABLE

We all have our haters, but when did you last take the opportunity to sit down in the Lord's presence and feast in the face of your enemies? The famous Psalm 23 says God has promised you a buffet of goodness in the face of your adversary, the devil.

As you bask in His presence, His anointing overflows on and in you until it spills out onto everyone around you. Your biggest cup will not hold all the goodness God is about to pour out on you in this season.

I don't know what you've been through in your life, but I do know if you're living, your life has not been perfect, and you have dealt with issues. The good news is that God has goodness and mercy locked on you like a heat-seeking missile. Your coordinates are always loaded into heaven's GPS. Expect His favor to explode all over you.

I am seated at the table of the Lord. I feast on His presence in the face of the enemies of fear, guilt, and shame. Everywhere I turn, Your goodness and mercy are hunting me down.

LORD, you alone are my portion and my cup; you make my lot secure. The boundary lines have fallen for me in pleasant places; surely I have a delightful inheritance.

PSALM 16:5–6, NIV

PROVISION AND FULFILLMENT

58

YOUR HEAVENLY PORTION

In an age when people get depressed comparing themselves to other people's "perfect" highlight reels on social media, we'd do well to remind ourselves that God has reserved us a heavenly portion.

That means He has a portion of goodness set aside for us only. It begins with recognizing that He, Himself, is our portion. He is the One who secures everything we will ever need. The boundary lines He has drawn around you give you access to an expansive and protected life.

When you're tempted to be stressed over your circumstances, remind yourself that you have an inheritance in the Lord. A man who knows his father has left him an inheritance isn't concerned with his temporal needs.

God has taken care of everything you need. When you pray, He doesn't have to leap off the throne to fulfill your request. He fashioned your solution long before you were even a baby in the womb. What a marvelous God we serve.

Jesus is my portion. He has an inheritance reserved just for me. I don't have to be jealous of someone else's blessing because the boundary lines of God's blessings for me are expansive.

They feast on the
abundance of
your house; you
give them drink
from your river of
delights. For with
you is the fountain
of life; . . .

PSALM 36:8–9, NIV

PROVISION AND FULFILLMENT

59

THE RIVER OF DELIGHT

So many of life's problems would be solved if we drank from the right source. The world gives us empty promises of fulfillment for which it doesn't and can't deliver. While the fountain of youth has been a sought-after fable in fairytales for generations, Scripture reveals its reality and location are with the Lord.

I started pondering how God wants us to eat of the abundance of His presence. It's not something He offers to us grudgingly. He wants us to drink our fill. God wants you to know true delight beyond the sinful pleasure that ends in guilt and shame.

Jesus is your fountain of life. Take advantage and drink until you are full!

Lord, show me the abundance of spending time in Your presence. I want to drink from the rivers of Your true pleasures, not the false substitutes the world offers. I drink of You, and I live.

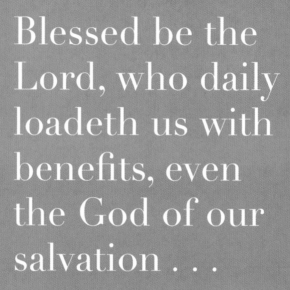

Blessed be the Lord, who daily loadeth us with benefits, even the God of our salvation . . .

PSALM 68:19, KJV

PROVISION AND FULFILLMENT

60

BENEFITS PACKAGE

Just like an employer offers employees a benefits package, Jesus has daily benefits for you to access. The word "loadeth" in this context implies an oversized portion poured out on your life.

This is one of our main motivations for blessing the Lord. We are filled with awe as we see His manifold grace express itself in different ways and areas in our daily lives. He is the God of our salvation. This bears repeating. Salvation is not just the initial born-again experience. It goes beyond that.

The word salvation in Hebrew in this verse is translated as yeshuah, meaning salvation, prosperity, deliverance, victory, etc. That sounds all-inclusive to me.

Don't allow the enemy to talk you down from your exalted status in Christ. By the blood of Jesus, you have a right to all the benefits of God's salvation package that Jesus died for you to have!

I have a heavenly benefits package that covers every area of my life. Jesus is my life's salvation. Amen.

The blessing of the LORD, it maketh rich, and he addeth no sorrow with it.

PROVERBS 10:22, KJV

PROVISION AND FULFILLMENT

61

THE BLESSING
OF THE LORD

When the Lord's blessing is on you, it makes you what you can't become in your own strength. Religious mindsets get offended when you start saying things like "God's blessing makes one rich," but it is recorded in Scripture in Proverbs 10:22.

God's definition of riches is different from the world's definition. He looks at the totality of life, not just at one piece. The world can promise riches, but it will come with sorrow. The reason for this is because if you get rich the world's way, you are doing it in your own power.

But God gives us a choice. We can come under His will and purpose and allow His blessing to make us everything we are called to be. If we choose to go the world's way, we may achieve a level of outward success, but it will come with a price.

As for me and my house, we will rest in God's goodness and blessings and trust in Him for everything we need.

I am blessed by God. He makes me rich in every area of my life. I choose God's road to wealth and not the world's compromising way, which adds sorrow.

Challenge your fears! Find your potential.

BISHOP T.D. JAKES

PROVISION AND FULFILLMENT

62

FACING FEAR

I remember when Serita and I moved to Dallas. We wanted to move into a certain neighborhood. What we didn't know at the time was that black people didn't typically move into that area.

Something happens when you aren't motivated by fear. Serita and I didn't know to be afraid. We just knew it was a nice place to live. We didn't put any limitations on ourselves. As a result, we broke a long-held barrier in that neighborhood by moving in when we did.

There are things that will challenge you. Don't let the voice of fear keep you locked in a place that God says you can go far beyond. Some of the best experiences we will ever have in this life will come on the other side of stepping out into the thing we fear. This is where God will reveal you to you. He wants to show you what you're made of because He knows what He's placed inside of you. Step out in bold faith and discover what God has known all along.

Father, I want to discover the good things you have on the other side of the fear that's tried to hinder me. Thank You for releasing my potential as I move forward into a fearless life.

A generous person will prosper; whoever refreshes others will be refreshed.

PROVERBS 11:25, NIV

PROVISION AND FULFILLMENT

63

THE GIVING SOUL

Generosity adds flavor to life. God thinks of our lives as flowing rivers. He wants His goodness to flow to us, but it's not meant to end there. He wants you to receive more than enough from Him so it can flow into the lives of other people.

Think of God as a river and a giver who wants to cultivate the same character in us. It is wonderful to be on the receiving end of a gift, but it is even more empowering to be the one who is doing the gift giving. Our world is full of thirsty souls. We encounter people every day who need a loving touch from God.

You're His representative. Ask God to show you how He wants to use you to be a blessing to others. He may lead you to pray for someone's healing or deliver an encouraging word. Just be open. As you walk the journey of the giving lifestyle, you will reap the rewards of growing in Christ's character.

Lord, thank You for giving me the heart of a giver. Show me how to refresh others in my daily life as a carrier of Your blessings.

"And you shall remember the LORD your God, for *it is* He who gives you power to get wealth, that He may establish His covenant which He swore to your fathers, as *it is* this day."

DEUTERONOMY 8:18, NKJV

PROVISION AND FULFILLMENT

64

COVENANT OF WEALTH

God doesn't have an issue with wealth. If He did, giving us the power to acquire it would be contradictory to His Word. From God's perspective, wealth touches every aspect of our lives—our spiritual lives, relationships, physical and emotional health, gifts and abilities, and our financial outlook.

The key to maintaining godly character as you manifest abundance is to remember God in all things. The world teaches us to forget about God as we ascend to higher levels of influence and blessing. When we forget God, wealth becomes a dangerous thing.

But for you, as a blood-bought child of God, your relationship with God makes you a candidate to walk in His blessings. He has made a covenant, and He will not forget His Word. Don't shrink back or be ashamed of God's blessing in your life. Jesus came to give you life and life more abundantly (John 10:10).

I have a covenant of wealth with Jesus Christ. That means nothing is missing or broken in my life. I do not forget the Lord who has blessed me with abundance.

But his delight is in the law of the LORD; and in his law doth he meditate day and night. And he shall be like a tree planted by the rivers of water, that bringeth forth his fruit in his season; his leaf also shall not wither; and whatsoever he doeth shall prosper.

PSALM 1:2–3, KJV

PROVISION AND FULFILLMENT

65

A FRUITFUL TREE

Developing a habit of meditating on the Word is one of the most life-giving things we can do. When fellowship with God moves from being a religious obligation to a living relationship, we begin to experience delight in our walk with God.

This causes us to grow deep roots. In the natural, when a tree is planted by the river, it's fed by a continuous source. The only thing it has to do is grow fruit. Our lives are like that. The more we are fed by God, the more fruit grows in our lives by default.

Jesus is the One who causes you to bear fruit in your due season. When we remain connected to the vine, our leaves stay vibrant. This means our souls are sound, our bodies are strong, and our relationships flourish.

God wants you to prosper in everything you do. He wants you to win. As you decide to abide in daily fellowship with Him, you will see the results of His fruit growing in your life.

Lord, help me to delight in fellowship with Your Word and in prayer. I ponder Your promises throughout my days, and I become fruitful like a well-watered tree.

Resist your fear.
It will never lead
you to a positive
end. Go after
your faith and
what you believe.

BISHOP T.D. JAKES

DYNAMIC FAITH

Health and Healing

Provision and Fulfillment

Soul Wellness

The Lord's Deliverance

Dynamic Faith

Purpose and Destiny

Contents

Dear Friend,

I'm overwhelmed as I reflect on how grateful I am to see another birthday. Thinking about all the Lord has done and allowed me to experience in 65 years reminds me that life always holds the potential for deeper insight and growth.

As I mature, the Lord has put a burning passion inside me to impart to as many others as I can everything He has revealed to me over the years. A life that is not shared is a life that is futile. We were created by a relational God who wants us to be a blessing to other people.

We put this special devotional together for that purpose. I want to pour out what I've received into your life. As I celebrate the Lord's goodness in my life, I want to impart a blessing to you. I want you to experience the fullness of your calling and purpose.

One thing I've learned over the past 65 years is that life truly begins when faith replaces fear as the major motivation in our lives. That's why I encourage you to go on a journey with me through 65 promises, insights, and blessings from God.

You are called to live a fulfilling life marked by love, purpose, and passion. I pray the Lord speaks to you as you journey through some of my favorite scriptures and spiritual nuggets God has revealed to me over the years.

Serita and I love you, and we are praying for you to experience the glories of God's peace, favor, and blessings!

Resting in His Promises,

T. D. Jakes